Journeying through covid:

Healed, Whole, and Worthy.

A 14-Day Survivor's Devotional and Journal

Rashad M. Roberts, MDiv

<u>**Contributors:**</u>

Dr. Kwabena Owusu-Boateng, DO
Family Medicine

Dr. Jessica Young Brown, PhD
Licensed Clinical Psychologist

<u>**Testimonials:**</u>

Raina Corbin

Vann Davis

Troy Wilkins

<u>**Resources:**</u>

www.webmd.com

my.clevelandclinic.org

cdc.gov/coronavirus/2019-ncov/index.html

www.medicalnewstoday.com

www.merriam-webster.com

www.biblegateway.com

Harrelson, W. (2003). *New interpreter's study bible: NRSV with Apocrypha*. Abingdon Press.

<u>**Cover Art**</u>
Samuel L. Roberts

<u>**Photograph**</u>
Gerald W. Holden

Contents

About the Author

Born and raised in Northern Virginia, Rashad M. Roberts matriculated through the Prince William County Public Schools. His relationship with God, love for music, and upbringing in the church have been driving forces. Rashad is a licensed minister and earned his Masters of Divinity, from the Samuel DeWitt Proctor School of Theology (STVU) on the campus of Virginia Union University in Richmond, VA. It was during his time there, and in a course called Spiritual Formation that he started doing the work to address his whole person (body, mind, and spirit). As he began this work, he became more vocal about the positive impact of combining Jesus and or faith and therapy. An advocate for mental health, the work of the church, the arts, youth, and young adults, he seeks to encourage individuals to begin their own process. Rashad has written in a journal since the age of 10; and as led, he does so to this day. He believes, there is power in our words, therefore there is power in the pen, and positive self-talk is necessary. It is his prayer that those who engage with his work, will come to this realization, and experience healing, wholeness, and a greater understanding of self-worth. The work continues…

The Professionals' Perspective

When it comes to covid like many other diseases, the best bet, is prevention.

Now that vaccines are available, the First step is to get vaccinated. This will prevent severe infection and make your symptoms manageable. Vaccinations and appropriate masking and social distance should help prevent the disease.

However, if you happen to still fall ill, please follow the guidelines below. Cover your mouth and nose with a tissue when you cough or sneeze. Wash your hands with soap and water for at least 20 seconds or clean your hands with an alcohol-based hand sanitizer that contains at least 60% alcohol covering all surfaces of your hands and rubbing them together after coughing or sneezing. Avoid touching your eyes, nose, and mouth with unwashed hands.

If you live with others, please clean all "high-touch" surfaces after use such as counters, tabletops, doorknobs, bathroom fixtures, toilets, phones, keyboards, tablets, and bedside tables. As well as any surface that might become contaminated.

Monitor your symptoms. Covid has the potential to infect every organ in your body, so monitoring your symptoms becomes very important. You need to know what you can handle at home and what needs medical attention. A mild cough, headache, fever that goes away with Tylenol is okay to manage at home. But chest pain, shortness of breath, swelling in legs, severe headaches, coughing up blood is not okay and you should seek medical help. And if unsure about what is normal, please contact your trusted health professional.

When it comes to quarantine it's a great time to do some self-reflection. Do not get into despair. I was once told by a covid positive patient that the worse thing about covid quarantine was loneliness and despair. She said your mind goes to a dark place while being alone. All that time spent alone and thinking about the what-ifs can play tricks on the mind. I suggest reaching out to friends or family, rediscovering an old hobby, starting a blog or vlog, spending time in your faith journey. As long as your symptoms allow you to. Covid is a viral disease and it will pass. Keep Tylenol, ibuprofen on hand for fevers, cough suppressants, get plenty of water and rest and you will make a full recovery.

A list of common symptoms and over the counter remedies:

Headache: Tylenol/ Ibuprofen/ Excedrin

Body Aches: Ibuprofen

Nausea: Zofran

Sore throat: Throat lozenges/ Halls

Coughing: Mucinex/ Robitussin

Fever: Tylenol/ Ibuprofen

Runny Nose: Flonase/ Afrin (3 days max use)

Loss of Taste and Smell: Smelling essential oils can help, but smell and taste in most cases return after illness

Dr. Kwabena B. Owusu-Boateng, DO
Family Medicine

Anxiety, Isolation, Overwhelm. The COVID-19 pandemic has stretched many of us to the edges of our sanity. In one sense, we've "all been in this together." In another, we've all been incredibly alone. We know that our human nature is oriented toward connection. We need others to be well, and God designed us to be in community. In this season though, the connection is exactly what put us at risk. The options that were safest for our physical health often put our mental health in jeopardy. For those of us who became ill with Covid, the primary instruction is hard to accept: isolation. In our moments of need, when we want *our* people, when we want to be comforted and cared for, it must be done from a distance. It's the right thing to do, but it's a hard thing to deal with.

Where is God in all of this? How do we reckon with all that we've lost, personally and collectively? How can we stand so much suffering, when there doesn't seem to be an end in sight? There are so many instances in the Bible when people felt all alone, and they called on God. Though this time has been challenging and overwhelming, we must remember that there is no situation so severe that God cannot reach us. Even when God doesn't make the situation go away, God is with us and God will see us through.

Consider this scripture from the fourth chapter of Philippians: "Do not worry about anything, but in everything by prayer and supplication with thanksgiving let your requests be made known to God. And the peace of God, which surpasses all understanding, will guard your hearts and your minds in Christ Jesus." (v4-6, NRSV)

Some of our religious experiences may have led us to believe that "Do not worry about anything" should be taken literally, causing us to feel shame when we feel upset, overwhelmed, and frustrated. But I think the invitation is to focus on the second clause of that sentence: **"in everything, by prayer and supplication, with thanksgiving, make your requests be made known to God."** No matter how we feel, no matter how bad it gets, it's always a good strategy to talk to God about it! In other words, you're upset, but you don't have to stay that way, because God will help you. Talking to God about our struggles has a few purposes. First, it allows us to acknowledge that we are not ok. Admitting to ourselves that we are in pain gives us the capacity to seek out our healing in ways that we can't when we are in denial. Second, we are empowered when we ask God to intervene in our situation. We serve a loving, compassionate God who is ready to come to our aid! Asking God for help engages our readiness to receive the help God is offering, whether that be an encouraging conversation with a friend, a devotional that comes at exactly the right time, or an appointment with a therapist to help you get on the right track. God is big enough and wide enough to send you help in all these ways! There is a third benefit to talking to God about our suffering: in exchange for our worries and requests, God grants us peace. This is not just any peace. It is peace so all-encompassing that we can't even understand it! What a relief! This peace is a balm, a comfort, that will guard our hearts and minds as we journey through the valley. It's not a band-aid, but it is a promise and a reminder that God is constantly working on our behalf, and wants us to feel whole.

Imagine those overwhelming feelings being a load that God wants to share. Are you willing to take EVERYTHING to God, and be open to solutions? Are you willing to admit that it feels bad so that you have the space to feel better? Can you admit if you've fallen apart so that you can be put back together again? Give it a try. The reward is indescribable peace!

Dr. Jessica Young Brown, PhD
Licensed Clinical Psychologist

Introduction

It was on Monday, November 9, 2020, that I first began to experience symptoms. Beginning with just a cough, and later I felt completely zapped. All of my energy was gone. On Thursday, November 12th, I was informed that someone from a singing engagement tested positive for covid. Immediately, I thought, oh this could be the reason why I wasn't well. Initially trying to schedule testing proved difficult, because of availability, in the height of the pandemic. However, on Saturday, November 14th I was able to schedule testing through the CVS minute clinic for Monday, November 16th. Still not feeling well and the list of symptoms growing, I drove up to the drive-thru and completed the nasal swab test, and awaited the results.

During this time, I also was able to schedule a Telemedicine appointment and it was clear based on the symptoms that it was either the flu or covid. The doctor conducting the exam prescribed some meds for the cough, body aches, and an antibiotic (Z pak). Nothing helped, but in fact, it grew increasingly worse. I went further into this spiral, a cyclone of sorts as I would describe. It was this feeling of slightly being lifted out of it one second, then immediately being dropped further into a dark space. There seemed to be no way out. Each new day I tried to remain hopeful that things would be different, but in fact, my reality was that I felt that I was going deeper into this unbelievable cycle.

Through the coughing, chills, fever, nausea, vomiting, the extreme fatigue, sweating, and loss of appetite; the loss of taste and smell, diarrhea, body aches, dehydration, headaches, anxiety, and difficulty breathing, I held on but my body and spirit were nudging me to make a move. I tried to manage it at home and found myself in search of relief sleeping on the hardwood floor of my upstairs hallway for two nights. On Thursday, November 19th (my mom's 60th birthday), I received a positive covid test result. I told myself that I would give it one more day and if there was no improvement, I was making my way to the hospital. On Friday, November 20th around 5:30 am I began searching for ways to get to the hospital without calling 911 for an ambulance. I was able to find a company that provided such services, but they did not have availability until the following week. I began to check Uber, but I saw a message regarding those experiencing symptoms to avoid using their service. I didn't want to use the service knowing that message was there. I looked at my Lyft app and there was no such message at that time and I booked a ride; making my way to INOVA Alexandria Hospital Emergency Room (ER). Before leaving I packed a couple of extra things in my backpack just in case, I wouldn't be returning home later that day. I made sure to have my mask, sanitizer/wipes and once the ride arrived, I got in the back passenger side and rolled down the window as a precaution. Once I arrived there was no one in the waiting area, so I was able to go straight back.

I'm so grateful I followed my gut (the Holy Spirit) and made the choice to check into the emergency room. After several hours in the emergency room, getting blood drawn, and another testing, EKG, x-ray, being on the not so comfortable gurney. Aside from having tested positive for covid, I found that I was extremely dehydrated, and also discovered that I had pneumonia in both lungs. In the ER, I was able to get fluids and antibiotics via Intravenous Injection (IV). That evening I was admitted and stayed there, for three days in room A2318. Saturday I was beginning to feel better than when I first arrived but not completely well, but better nonetheless. I rested in my hospital bed, took meds, as given such as a blood thinner to prevent clotting, and a steroid. For three days I did this but received word of my possible discharge on Saturday evening for some time Sunday. I was ecstatic and grateful knowing that I was in place and felt well "enough" to return home.

I was hopeful that my condition would continue to improve. This especially being true, I have stayed on top of the meds prescribed, hydrated, checked temperature regularly, ate even if there was no real appetite, and did the breathing exercises. There was indeed hope because of my hope in Jesus as throughout the ordeal, JESUS stayed on my lips. I didn't have many words to utter but believe as I spoke the name Jesus, he heard my cry and understood my groaning as to what the need was. There had to be a shift in my thoughts to match the confession. That shift occurred when I began to think of the testimony this would be and the inspiration it could provide to others of the healing power of Jesus and that God and medicine work together and are not mutually exclusive. The testimony would be that what was, is no longer. One of healing, wholeness, and worth; and increased faith in the power of God.

I am still recovering and praying for my complete healing. I would like to get tested again, but the cough needs to be gone before that. I know I haven't made it to this point on my prayers alone, but there has been a group of folks calling out my name. For their concern and care to pray I am grateful. I am grateful for those who reached out offering to help where needed. These acts of kindness are not only acknowledged but accepted. The acceptance of help is not always the easiest for me, but in this place, I was to receive the love and extended hands that reached out in care. That's just an extension of God's love that we as believers should display one to another as communities of faith.

My declaration has been and will be that I Believe! I am Healed, Whole, and Worthy!

This is also my prayer for you, that you will keep the faith to believe, that you are healed, whole, and worthy.

Rashad's Personal Journal Entry
November 24, 2020

In response to my experience with covid, I felt led to compile this devotional and journal, as a source of encouragement and hope in a unique way. Though I survived this ordeal, after being released from the hospital, for days, weeks, and even months, I had high anxiety. I could not rest as my body was still adjusting; and the thought of death was constant. Everyone's experience is different, from very minor to very severe. This book is based upon the initial Centers for Disease Control (CDC) guidelines to quarantine for 14 days. Maybe you've received a positive covid test result and going through your own ordeal, or have decided to quarantine as a precaution, or you're a supportive family member or friend; as you journey doing your work, keep the faith. Make an effort to think on the good even when faced with the most challenging of times. This is not to ignore where you are at the moment, but to acknowledge, address it, and shift your perspective to the possibilities of what can be. This is easier said than done, and requires work, but it is possible. As you read the devotions, heed advice from professionals, pray, reflect and write your thoughts, use the at-home treatments for immediate symptoms, listen to the free playlists provided, self –assess to gauge where you are and what you are feeling on any given day, or gain strength from the testimonies of others, know you are worthy of this work. I have intentionally written covid or covid-19 in lowercase as I did during my experience as a way to diminish its power. It is my prayer that you would begin to speak positively over yourself and your current state. And by faith, believe that what is will not always be, for trouble won't last always and better days are ahead.

14-Day Devotional

I Believe! I am Healed, Whole, and Worthy.

Symptom: Cough

At-Home Treatment: 1. A teaspoon or two of honey may cut mucus production. Honey also kills germs. But remember, it can cause botulism, a rare form of food poisoning, in babies. Never give it to any child younger than 1. **2.** Breathing in steam may help with coughing because it calms and moisturizes your airways. You can also add essential oils like peppermint to the water for extra comfort. 3. Hot drinks won't ease a stuffy head, but they can soothe a cough much better than room temperature drinks. Sip on hot tea or water if you're seeking relief.

<u>Our Hope:</u> <u>We are Healed</u>

Scripture: *"But he was wounded for our transgressions, crushed for our iniquities; upon him was the punishment that made us whole, and by his bruises, we are healed."* Isaiah 53:5 NRSV

The Prophet Isaiah in this 53rd chapter and 5th verse has some words that speak to the restoration of the Israelites from exile, back to Jerusalem. In this passage, he speaks of the work of one who was not looked upon favorably or in admiration but rather discarded was sent to accomplish. Yes, God has brought you Israelites from exile, making you a whole nation, but there is one destined to make you whole people. A restorer whose name is Jesus.

The restorer has taken on the punishment of the cross to bring healing and make us whole. As you begin to acknowledge what is happening within your body, today maybe it's a cough that has come from out of nowhere or maybe you know exactly how you may have contracted the virus or just simply taking precautions. Remember that while Isaiah prophesied of the restorer's work, this restoration is present. There is restoration for your soul through the work of the cross, but also your body. How you and your soul experience this present life was on the mind of God when Jesus was sent into the earth. And now the work is complete and we can proclaim our healing because of Jesus' endurance to withstand crucifixion; being bruised, crushed, pierced in his side, receiving a crown of thorns, nails in his hands, and feet, that where you are right now, you can declare I AM HEALED. Speak it, Write it, Reflect on it. I AM HEALED.

20

Prayer:

Most gracious and eternal Lord, we are so grateful for the gift of your son Jesus who was prophesied and came to restore us; that we may receive the wholeness that is in you. Because of your restorative work we can now prophesy over ourselves and also receive our healing, as Isaiah wrote in the 53rd chapter. So, we call it by faith, I am Healed, Whole, and Worthy in the name of Jesus.

Honest Self-Assessment

Devotional Reflection:

____

____

____

____

____

____

____

How do you feel in body, mind, and spirit?

____

____

____

____

____

____

____

<u>**What are you speaking over yourself today?**</u>

____
23
____

____

____

____

____

____

I Believe! I am Healed, Whole, and Worthy.

Symptom: Fever

Your body may raise its temperature to help you fight off an infection. When your body is hotter, it makes it harder for viruses or bacteria to survive. The fever also tells your immune system to make more white blood cells join in the fight. So, a fever may help protect you, even if it makes you feel worse for a little while

At-Home Treatment: Studies show that people may be slightly cooler, so the norm is anywhere between 97 and 99 F. Over-the-counter medicines like acetaminophen and ibuprofen may ease a fever in adults and children older than 6 months. Adults can use aspirin, but never give it to children. Lighter clothes may help. A light blanket and drinking cool liquids could also. A lukewarm shower, bath, or sponge bath may also help people cool down.

Our Hope: All is Well

Scripture: *"Beloved, I pray that all may go well with you and that you may be in good health, just as it is well with your soul."*
3 John 1:2 NRSV

This third letter of John was written to a leader of a congregation in praise of their faithfulness in walking in the truth. The truth being of their revelation of God in Christ.

On this day as you think of your current state, your past, and the future ahead, remember God rewards those who are faithful and will cause all to be well with you. This includes your health. While Jesus came to save your soul, he is as concerned with your bodily health and desires for you to be well and in good health. Well, what is good about where I am currently you may ask. And I believe that the condition in which you face now is not the end. In the not-so-distant future, I believe that the words of this text will be your testimony. Just Hold On!

Maybe your temperature has risen and you would love for it to break, understand that a fever is also a way in which your body fights infection, and as your body fights, the fever will soon break. The fever is protection, even though you may feel bad for a little.

I believe the Lord is saying, as you remain steadfast in the truth, this will be my praise, my reward to you for your faithfulness; wellness and good health will be yours, as it is well with your soul.

Stay faithful to the truth that you know and call it forth over your life. I AM Healed Whole, and WORTHY.

Prayer:

To the God who will turn my current state into a testimony of praise, I give you thanks. You are good and I am grateful that just as you care for my soul, that you care for my body, and as today's scripture has reminded, that it is desired that all will be well with me and I will be in good health, just as it is well with my soul. By the truth of my faith in you, I Am Healed, Whole, and Worthy. All is well in the name of Jesus.

<u>Devotional Reflection:</u>

____

____

____

____

____

____

____

<u>How do you feel in body, mind, and spirit?</u>

____

____

____

____

____

____

____

____

____

____

____

____

____

____

I Believe! I am Healed, Whole, and Worthy.

Symptom: Chills

At-Home Treatment: Layering clothes or getting to a warm place can make cold chills go away. You can also drink hot chocolate, coffee, or tea to raise your internal body temperature. If an illness, infection, or another health problem causes chills, treating the condition should get rid of the symptom. Treatments vary depending on the underlying cause. They may include:

- Antibiotics for bacterial and parasitic infections.

- Antiviral medications for viral infections.

- Over-the-counter medicine, such as acetaminophen (Tylenol®) or ibuprofen (Advil®), for conditions like flu that cause fevers and chills.

<h2><u>Our Hope:</u> <u>Think on These</u></h2>

Scripture: *Finally, beloved, whatever is true, whatever is honorable, whatever is just, whatever is pure, whatever is pleasing, whatever is commendable, if there is any excellence and if there is anything worthy of praise, think about these things. Keep on doing the things that you have learned and received and heard and seen in me, and the God of peace will be with you.* Philippians 4:8-9 NRSV

In this final letter to the church at Philippi, Paul encourages them in verses 8 & 9 to think about what they know of truth, honor, justice, purity, pleasing to God, and commendable; any and everything worth praise, to give thought to those things. And to continue doing what they have seen him exemplify.

When we're sick and our bodies are going through the effects of a viral infection, it is often difficult to maintain a positive outlook. It's not that is impossible but it does take some training. Therefore, as you go through this trial, you may have a moment or two, or three, where thinking on these things as Paul described and even prescribed for us, does not come easy. However, in the training of our thoughts, we need to do what we can to counter thoughts that are not true, not honorable, just, pure, or pleasing, etc. For instance, a thought may come that says this sickness is unto death, bring that thought captive by the truth that is in scripture that says," I shall not die, but live to declare the works of Lord." Psalm 118: 17 NKJV This is what I believe we are to learn here as well as to see the example of other believers as they contended in the faith, and knowing that witnesses before them also provided an example of how to endure. Recall the lessons, of your parents, grandparents, aunts, uncles, maybe there is a brother or sister or even a friend that has endured some tough times and come out on the other side. If not, we can recount the lessons found in scripture from the lives of those such as Moses, Job, Ruth, Naomi, Deborah, Jeremiah, Paul, the centurion soldier, Mary, and Martha (sisters of Lazarus), and even Jesus himself. As you do this, you will be reminded that the God of peace is with you. You are not in this alone and you can make it. Think on what is true, what is honorable, what is just, what is pure, what is pleasing, what is commendable and worthy of praise. Think on these.

Prayer:

Thank you, Lord, for the ability to think and decipher what is true and pure as a believer. When negative thoughts come, Lord help me to remember who you are, and have been to not only others but who I have experienced you to be. Let this kind of thinking permeate my being and grant me the peace of your presence; giving me the assurance that I will endure and that my declaration will be made manifest. I am healed, whole, and worthy, in Jesus' name.

Honest Self-Assessment

Devotional Reflection:

____

____

____

____

____

____

____

How do you feel in body, mind, and spirit?

____

____

____

____

____

____

____

<u>**What are you speaking over yourself today?**</u>

I Believe! I am Healed, Whole, and Worthy.

Symptom: Loss of Appetite (Unable to Taste or Smell)

At-Home Treatment: eat whatever is appealing. Some other tips to help you control nausea include:

- Eat small, frequent meals throughout the day if an empty stomach makes you nauseous
- Sip cold, clear liquids throughout the day
- Avoid fatty, fried, spicy, or greasy foods
- Try eating your food at room temperature or cold to decrease any strong smells
- Eat bland foods such as crackers
- Suck on hard candies such as mints or sour candy to get rid of smells that bother you
- Eat popsicles or gelatin if you can't keep anything else down

<u>Our Hope:</u> <u>The Lord Who Heals</u>

Scripture: *"...for I am the Lord who heals you."* Exodus 15:26 NRSV

Moses in this 15th chapter of Exodus has cried out to God after three days in the wilderness and no safe drinking water. The water of Mariah was bitter and contaminated but through Moses' prayer and obedience, God made that same water sweet to taste. In this verse, Moses was assured that if he listens to the voice of the Lord and does what's right, the disease brought on the Egyptians will not befall him, "for I am the Lord who heals you."

While you may be experiencing a loss of taste, the savory and sweet flavors of your favorite foods are gone, your appetite waning, your sense of smell may be extremely sensitive or you may not be able to smell at all, in fact, you may no longer even have an appetite. Know that this is temporary, just as Moses cried out to God, use this as an opportunity for you to do the same. Cry out to God regarding your current state believing that God can turn a bitter situation into something sweet. Showing forth God's healing hand and restoration of the senses. In your crying out understand that it's not anything in particular that you may have done to bring this on, but as a believer, a part of doing right in God's sight is trusting God by crying out in prayer. On the other hand, it is times like this that also may open communication with God that may have been lacking and this time may be used to get our attention. This also requires us to recognize our own limitations and understand that complete healing is available, "for I am the Lord who heals you." the Lord who heals translated in the Hebrew, Jehovah-Rapha (more properly Yahweh-Rapha) Cry out, I AM Healed, Whole, and Worthy.

Prayer:

God as you were there for Moses, I believe that you are present and able to heal me. You can restore my appetite as well as my senses that I taste and know the difference between bitter and sweet. The senses allow me to partake in a meal and enjoy it. I cry out to you Jehovah-Rapha and my confession is that I am healed, whole, and worthy by the hand of the Lord who ME. In Jesus' name, Amen.

Honest Self-Assessment

Devotional Reflection:

____

____

____

____

____

____

____

How do you feel in body, mind, and spirit?

____

____

____

____

____

____

____

<u>**What are you speaking over yourself today?**</u>

____

____

____

____

____

____

____

I Believe! I am Healed Whole, and Worthy.

Symptom: Fatigue

At-Home Treatment: 1. Look at your situation. Evaluate your level of energy. Be alert to your warning signs of fatigue. Fatigue warning signs may include tired eyes, tired legs, whole-body tiredness, stiff shoulders, decreased energy or a lack of energy, inability to concentrate, weakness or malaise, boredom or lack of motivation, sleepiness, increased irritability, nervousness, anxiety, or impatience. 2. Conserve your energy. Pace yourself. A moderate pace is better than rushing through activities. Keep sudden or prolonged strains to a minimum. Alternate sitting and standing. Limit work that requires reaching over your head. For example, use long-handled tools, store items lower, and delegate activities whenever possible. Limit work that makes muscles tense. 3. Eat Right. Fatigue is often made worse if you don't eat enough or if you don't choose the right foods. Maintaining good nutrition can help you feel better and have more energy. 4. Exercise. A drop in physical activity, which may be the result of illness or treatment, can lead to tiredness and lack of energy. Regular, moderate exercise can keep these feelings away, help you stay active, and give you more energy. 5. Learn to manage stress. Managing stress can play an important role in combating fatigue. Try relaxation techniques. Audiotapes that teach deep breathing or visualization can help ease stress. Do things that divert your attention away from fatigue. For example, knitting, reading, or listening to music don't use up physical energy but require attention. If your stress seems out of control, talk to your doctor. They are there to help.

<u>Our Hope:</u> <u>Rest</u>

Scripture: *"For surely I know the plans I have for you, says the Lord, plans for your welfare and not for harm, to give you a future with hope."* Jeremiah 29:11 NRSV

Yesterday, we took into consideration various thoughts that may flood our mind, when sick and the idea of training our thoughts. Know that there may come a time along your journey when you may not give much thought to anything except to get from one moment to the next. During these times, we can use this verse in the 29th chapter of Jeremiah, that when we can't think for ourselves, God has thoughts for us. In the New Revised Standard Version, the word "plan" is used whereas in the New King James Version "thought" is. Either word should encourage us that there is a plan, there are thoughts, that you are on the mind of God. That when you can't think for yourself, that God's thoughts, God's plan is for your welfare and not harm, and that you have a future filled with hope. So as your body lacks the energy to contend with the responsibilities of the day, take a rest in the plan and thoughts that God has for you. I don't know of a better way to rest than knowing that the creator of all things has already gone before you, covering you, and has a plan for your successful outcome. Know that in those thoughts you are healed, whole, and worthy.

Prayer:

God, this day I don't have many words but I trust that you know what I am going through. Continue to cover me and keep me in your thoughts, that I may know your goodness through my healing and you may get the glory. In the name of Jesus, Amen.

<u>Honest Self-Assessment</u>

<u>Devotional Reflection:</u>

____

____

____

____

____

____

<u>How do you feel in body, mind, and spirit?</u>

____

____

____

____

____

____

____

____

____

____

____

____

____

I Believe! I am Healed, Whole, and Worthy.

Symptom: Congestion

At-Home Treatment: Use a humidifier or vaporizer.

- Take long showers or breathe in steam from a pot of warm (but not too hot) water.
- Drink lots of fluids. This will thin out your mucus, which could help prevent blocked sinuses.
- Use a nasal saline spray. It's salt water, and it will help keep your nasal passages from drying out.
- Try a **Neti pot**, nasal irrigator, or bulb syringe. Use distilled, sterile water or H2O that's been boiled and cooled to make up the irrigation solution. Rinse the irrigation device after each use and let it air dry.
- Place a warm, wet towel on your face. It may relieve discomfort and open your nasal passages.
- Prop yourself up. At night, lie on a couple of pillows. Keeping your head elevated may make breathing more comfortable.
- Use **lozenges** to keep your throat moist.
- Use **bronchodilators**, which relax the muscles in your lungs and widen your bronchi to make breathing easier. Bronchodilators are often used to treat long-term conditions where your airways become inflamed and narrow, such as **asthma**.
- Avoid chlorinated pools. They can irritate your nasal passages.
- Blow your nose the right way: gently, so you don't force mucus into your ears or other parts of your sinuses, into a disposable tissue so you don't spread germs. Wash your hands afterward.

<u>Our Hope:</u> <u>Say It and Believe</u>

Scripture: *"Truly I tell you, if you say to this mountain, 'Be taken up and thrown into the sea, and if you do not doubt in your heart, but believe that what you say will come to pass, it will be done for you. So I tell you, whatever you ask for in prayer, believe that you have received it, and it will be yours."* Mark 11: 23-24 NRSV

The entire bible is filled with faith-filled stories and instructions for how we take what is written and bring it to life. In this faith journey, we may not always believe 100% that which we have read because we haven't experienced or seen the miracle of the mountain being removed as referenced here, firsthand. As we aim to grow in our faith and see the light in what may be a dark situation, we must put to practice saying what we see and or desire before it comes to pass. The repetition of constantly speaking will foster growth in our belief that what we have been given the authority to speak, will manifest. The mountain of the challenges faced due to covid can be the miracle of our healing as we speak to it in faith. This is a lesson I learned for myself that as I constantly spoke over myself and my belief in the God who was able to do it, the more I felt the meter moved in the direction of the healing I desired. Healing by the power of God from the words I've spoken came to life and became my testimony. The mountain can be moved and the miracle yours. Say it, I am healed, whole, and worthy.

Prayer:

Thank you, God, for the ability to use my words in faith to speak to circumstances and situations. It is my desire that doubt is removed and my belief in your ability as the sovereign God will continue to grow. As I speak my healing and ask for it in prayer, I believe that which is spoken I will also receive, in the name of Jesus. Amen.

Honest Self-Assessment

Devotional Reflection:

____

____

____

____

____

____

____

How do you feel in body, mind, and spirit?

____

____

____

____

____

____

I Believe! I am Healed, Whole, and Worthy.

Symptom: Nausea/Vomiting

At-Home Treatment: Ginger has been used for thousands of years to reduce pain and stomach ills. Researchers believe the chemicals in ginger work in the stomach and intestines as well as the brain and nervous system to control nausea.

<u>Our Hope:</u> <u>There is Peace</u>

Scripture: *"Do not worry about anything, but in everything by prayer and supplication with thanksgiving let your requests be made known to God. And the peace of God, which surpasses all understanding, will guard your hearts and your minds in Christ Jesus."*
Philippians 4: 6-7 NRSV

In the earlier stages of the covid pandemic and through my hospitalization it was made evident how important an individual's mental state was. Persons battling the virus were fighting its effects not only physically but that physical battle became a battle of the mind, so much so they contemplated suicide. Every time a nurse, technician, or doctor visited my room, even from the point of my arrival in the ER, I was asked, "do you have thoughts of hurting yourself?". Each time they asked I found myself giving thanks, that I had no such thoughts, and continued to pray that God would guard my heart and mind, placing my hand on my head and heart. This passage became a constant source of encouragement to release my cares to the Lord, giving way for God's peace to meet me in a way that my confidence in God's abilities surpassed what I was currently facing. It would be the peace of God, that would guard my heart and mind in Christ Jesus. I was grateful, that I had the mental capacity to understand what was taking place but also an awareness of the road that I did not desire to go down. This awareness kept me in a cycle of prayerful gratitude, releasing my concerns and giving thanks; as I found the good in what did not look so good, but also giving thanks in advance in the expectation of being healed, made whole, and worth the fight. That is my prayer for you, that you acknowledge your limitations, and release that which is out of your control to God, and that he may grant you peace, guarding your heart and mind, that you are not consumed, but confident that God is able.

Prayer:

Most gracious and eternal Lord, I thank you now for your peace. The peace that allows me, in the face of adversity, to release my concerns, and say confidently, that you've got it and you've got me. God, you're in control and in your care, I am covered. My heart and mind are secured in your peace. In Jesus' name. Amen.

Honest Self-Assessment

Devotional Reflection:

____

____

____

____

____

____

____

How do you feel in body, mind, and spirit?

____

____

____

____

____

____

____

I Believe! I am Healed, Whole, and Worthy.

Symptom: Night Sweats

At-Home Treatment: Non-drug treatments for night sweats from any cause include:

- Wearing loose-fitting, lightweight, cotton pajamas
- Using layered bedding that can be removed as needed during the night
- Turning on a bedroom fan/opening windows
- Sipping cool water throughout the night
- Keeping a cold pack under a pillow, then turning your pillow over to rest your head on a cool surface
- Avoiding common night sweat triggers such as alcohol, spicy foods, caffeine, cigarettes
- De-stressing through deep breathing, relaxation, and exercise
- Undergoing hypnosis to help relax and focus on feeling cool
- Exercising daily. Walking, swimming, dancing, and bicycling are all good choices.

<u>Our Hope:</u> <u>Hope to Believe in</u>

Scripture: *"May the God of hope fill you with all joy and peace in believing, so that you may abound in hope by the power of the Holy Spirit."* Romans 15:13 NRSV

In the 15th Chapter of Romans, Paul addresses how the Gospel is true for the Jew and the Gentile. Therefore, God's promises are not reserved only to the patriarchs who were Jewish, but now through Jesus' ministry, they are extended to the Gentiles, as they receive salvation. The 13th verse of this chapter is a blessing Paul writes in regards to the new life of Christ.

When I first began to experience symptoms and then to get the positive test result for covid, my mind became filled with thoughts of news headlines, those who were hospitalized, the number of people who had passed, the people I knew that experienced hospitalization, and also death due to this virus or complications the virus caused those with underlying issues. I was brought to this scripture passage that speaks of hope. Hope is defined as wanting something to happen or be true, and to think it can happen or be true. As believers in Christ, we have this promise that we can experience a life of abundance and that's not only material things, but that takes into account your health; your physical, mental, and spiritual state. And having considered your whole being, Paul is inspired to write this blessing, that you are filled with joy and peace in believing, so that you may abound in hope. That by hope you live and tackle life's obstacles, even if your physical condition, won't allow you, the spirit of God the hope of glory is in you and fights for you, that you are not over taken by it, but you know your healing is possible, and sickness is overcome by the power of the Holy Spirit. Your healing is true, your wholeness is true, and yes you, even you, are worthy to receive it.

Prayer:

My hope is built on nothing less, than Jesus' blood and righteousness, God, we thank you for this reminder of the Hope we have in you. Help us now in moments of doubt to hold fast to this truth of that which you have spoken and even that which we desire can be our reality. Help us to hold on to hope that allows us to declare we are healed, whole, and worthy by the power of the Holy Spirit. In Jesus' name. Amen.

<u>**Honest Self-Assessment**</u>

<u>**Devotional Reflection:**</u>

____

____

____

____

____

____

____

<u>**How do you feel in body, mind, and spirit?**</u>

____

____

____

____

____

____

____

____

____

____

____

____

____

____

I Believe! I am Healed, Whole, and Worthy.

Symptom: Diarrhea

At-Home Treatment: If your case is mild, you may not need to take anything. Adults can take an over-the-counter medicine such as **bismuth** subsalicylate or **loperamide**, which you can get as liquids or tablets. You also need to stay hydrated. You should drink at least six 8-ounce glasses of fluids each day. Choose electrolyte replacement drinks or soda without **caffeine**. Chicken broth (without the **fat**), **tea** with honey, and sports drinks are also good choices. Instead of drinking liquids with your meals, drink liquids between meals. Sip small amounts of fluids often. **Liquid probiotics** may also help.

<u>Our Hope:</u> <u>Write the Vision</u>

Scripture: *"Then the Lord answered me and said: Write the vision; make it plain on tablets, so that a runner may read it. For there is still a vision for the appointed time; it speaks of the end and does not lie. If it seems to tarry, wait for it; it will surely come, it will not delay. Look at the proud. Their spirit is not right in them, but the righteous live by their faith."* Habakkuk 2:2-4 NRSV

In Habakkuk the 1st Chapter, Habakkuk is making complaints regarding the moral and social order breakdown but also the slack that he sees in law and failure of justice. These complaints become a back and forth between him and God. When we get to the 2nd Chapter of Habakkuk, he is keeping watch and awaiting God's response. God's response is for him to write the vision on tablets, the vision being to address what is currently happening, and what the ideal resolution would be. How would the law be enforced and what would justice look like? Just also referring to righteousness, those who were causing the chaos would be considered the proud in this text, but those wanting to keep the order are righteous. The righteous are visionaries and live by their faith.

A major component of this devotional is that it is also a journal. Writing our thoughts down, how we're feeling, what has gotten under our skin, what's tapping on our last nerve, the things going on in our lives (what is the chaos that has entered our space), and those things that we are believing for in faith (what is it that we see is our outcome). It is my prayer that having space to reflect and check with yourself by writing your thoughts down, your faith thoughts down will aid you in not becoming bogged down by what is happening now, but the expectation that what is happening will not always be and better is before you. Though the vision of what is to come seems to be taking its time, continue to live by faith, because there is an end to your current condition. Once it comes at its appropriate time, it going to be quick and you may wonder how, but by accounting for where you've been and what you've experienced, you will know. It was the written vision, spoken word, and ultimately, the Lord being your help.

Prayer:

Most gracious and eternal Lord, I am grateful that I can see a thing before I see it. Thank you for the gift of vision and faith, that would cause me to trust you and believe that the vision will come to pass. God at this time the vision I call forth and write in faith is that I am healed, whole, and worthy. In Jesus' name. Amen.

Honest Self-Assessment

Devotional Reflection:

____

____

____

____

____

____

____

How do you feel in body, mind, and spirit?

____

____

____

____

____

____

____

I Believe! I am Healed, Whole, and Worthy.

Symptom: Body Aches

At-Home Treatment: Essential oils such as Lavender, Rosemary, Peppermint, and Eucalyptus may reduce pain as well as inflammation. Ginger and Turmeric have pain-relieving qualities. NSAIDs (nonsteroidal anti-inflammatory drugs**).** This group of meds includes aspirin, ibuprofen, and naproxen. Each is different, but they all reduce fevers and pain. NSAIDs may work better than acetaminophen at lowering a fever. Check with your doctor before you use NSAIDs if you have a history of stomach problems, heart, liver, or kidney disease, or if you're taking a blood thinner.

<u>Our Hope:</u> <u>Grace for Hope</u>

Scripture: *"Therefore, since we are justified by faith, we have peace with God through our Lord Jesus Christ, 2 through whom we have obtained access[b] to this grace in which we stand; and we[c] boast in our hope of sharing the glory of God. 3 And not only that, but we also boast in our sufferings, knowing that suffering produces endurance, 4 and endurance produces character, and character produces hope, 5 and hope does not disappoint us, because God's love has been poured into our hearts through the Holy Spirit that has been given to us."*
Romans 5:1-5 NRSV

Verses 1-5 of the 5th Chapter of Romans speak of the suffering that we may have to endure but in our enduring the suffering, what the believer can expect. The work of Jesus at this time is complete and has given us access to grace that in common language will allow us to go through difficult times and not look like what we've been through.

Christ's suffering and endurance on the cross have not only granted us grace, but it has also provided an example and set for us an expectation. The cross and Christ's suffering have given us grace through faith to all who believe. This work has also provided an example of how one can withstand the most tumultuous times and come out on the other side an even better version of themselves. In addition, it has given us an expectation of hope through the Holy Spirit. As believers being filled with the power of God's Spirit, we have peace with God. And that hope sets our expectation that if we find ourselves in a state of suffering, we can expect endurance, and endurance will produce character, and character produces hope.

Hope that we can boast in, because we stand on the completed work of Jesus, the grace extended to us and knowing it to be true. Know that as you go through this time understand, the work will be completed in you, your endurance may be developing, endurance may develop your character, and character developing and solidifying hope in you through the Holy Spirit; therefore, you are healed, whole, and worthy. Grace for Hope.

Prayer:

For the grace given us through the sacrifice of your son, thank you, Lord. I thank you that through his sacrifice the work is complete and that as I endure this trial, character, and hope are being developed in me. My life will be an even brighter light for both the believer and non-believer. Continue to cover me and cause me to stand in Your grace and truth. It's in Jesus' name I pray. Amen.

Devotional Reflection:

____

____

____

____

____

____

____

How do you feel in body, mind, and spirit?

____

____

____

____

____

____

____

____

____

____

____

____

____

I Believe! I am Healed, Whole, and Worthy.

Symptom: Dehydration

At-Home Treatment: The best way to avoid **dehydration** is to drink plenty of fluids, especially if you're in a hot climate or you're playing or working in the sun. Be aware of how much fluid you're losing through sweat and when you pee. Drink enough to keep up with what you're getting rid of. You can also lose necessary fluids more quickly than normal when you have a **high fever, diarrhea,** or are throwing up. As your body loses fluids, it also loses **electrolytes**. These are **minerals** in your **blood** and body fluids that affect how your muscles and nerves work. When you lose electrolytes, you need to replace them. There are many over-the-counter products for doing this. Most people get these through their regular meals by eating meats, vegetables, and fruits. But there are also sports drinks, gels, candies and gummies you can take. There's even a tablet that you can dissolve in water and drink.

<u>Our Hope:</u> <u>Glory Revealed</u>

Scripture: *"I consider that the sufferings of this present time are not worth comparing with the glory about to be revealed to us."*
Romans 8:18 NRSV

As you take a moment this day acknowledge that you are the glory of God. Your suffering, your tears, your frustration, the ups and downs of this journey are not in vain but for the glory that is about to be revealed not only to us but also "...in us." (NKJV). While it has been difficult to know that your time in isolation was also a time in which God could have you alone without outside noise or distractions to work on you, allowing you to draw closer and that you may be revealed as a testimony to the work of the Holy Spirit and witness of God's glory in the earth. You are the manifest presence of God. God's spirit alive in you has brought you from a dark place and now your light will shine causing men and women to glorify God in heaven. Though we have to endure hard times, if we can alter our perspective to know that while it concerns us, it is also so much bigger than us, and ultimately for the edifying of the body of believers and God's glory.

Prayer:

God these days have been some of the most difficult that I've faced and at times I don't understand what it's all about. At those moments Lord and right now cause me to recognize that it's always bigger than me and that I'm just a part of the larger work you are doing. That through the suffering, I'm being changed and your glory will be revealed. In Jesus's name. Amen.

Honest Self-Assessment

Devotional Reflection:

____

____

____

____

____

____

____

How do you feel in body, mind, and spirit?

____

____

____

____

____

____

____

<u>**What are you speaking over yourself today?**</u>

I Believe! I am Healed, Whole, and Worthy.

Symptom: Headache

At-Home Treatment: When it comes to **headache** remedies, medications and others can help prevent headaches from starting, but they aren't the only option. Changing your lifestyle to control stress or avoid triggers may work well, too. These tactics may even prevent you from getting headaches. What works for one person may not work for another, so talk to your doctor to figure out the best remedy for you. Try these simple things to help yourself feel better:

- Use an ice pack on your forehead, scalp, or neck.

- Take OTC meds like acetaminophen, ibuprofen, or naproxen.

- Get some caffeine.

- Go to a dark, quiet room.

- Peppermint Oil The active ingredient in peppermint is menthol. Some small studies show it can lessen the pain of migraine headaches. It may also reduce other symptoms like light sensitivity, nausea, and vomiting. A few studies suggest that applying a peppermint oil solution to your forehead and temples can help take away tension headaches, too.

<u>Our Hope:</u> <u>Why I Let You Live</u>

Scripture: *"But this is why I have let you live: to show you my power, and to make my name resound through all the earth"*
Exodus 9:16 NRSV

At the top of the 9th chapter of Exodus, the 5th Plague of Livestock Diseased is commenced after Pharaoh refused to let the Israelites go. The plagues continued as Pharaoh persisted to refuse the command received by Moses with the sixth being Boils and the seventh of Thunder and Hail. There have been those that have compared the covid pandemic to the times of plague in biblical times. The countless people afflicted and the number of lives lost seems to be of biblical proportions but I personally cannot say with assurance why God has allowed such. What I do know is that, what God has allowed is out of our control, however what is not, is how we respond. In reading the 16th verse of this 9th chapter of Exodus, I found great encouragement. Yes, this verse was addressing pharaoh and neither you nor I am that, but when I read these words alone, I found hope. "But this is why I let you live…" Yes, there seems to be despair, destruction, and desolation around, and you've borne witness to some terrible things, but you are alive. Alive right here and now and in your living, while you've seen the turbulence of the times, you have also seen the grace for living. You've seen the lives that have been healed, you've seen lives that have flourished, you've seen the mending of broken relationships, you've seen and received help from some unexpected sources. It hasn't all been bad, but in God allowing you to live, you have seen God's power, and you have graced to live to make sure the name of Lord resound through all the earth. You are not only a survivor but an overcomer, who has been graced for this season. But this is why I let you live…Live and allow your life to resound (sound loudly, produce sonorous or echoing sound) reverberate, healed, whole, and worthy.

"Glad to be in the service, Glad to be in the service, Glad to be in the service one more time. He didn't have to let me live; He didn't have to let me live. Live to be in the service one more time."

Prayer:

For the mercy that is new every morning and the grace extended to me through faith, God, I thank you for letting me Live. It is my prayer that as your spirit lives in me, it will cause my life to shine in a way that your great name echoes through the earth. In the name of Jesus. Amen.

<u>**Honest Self-Assessment**</u>

<u>**Devotional Reflection:**</u>

<u>**How do you feel in body, mind, and spirit?**</u>

<u>**What are you speaking over yourself today?**</u>

____

____

____

____

____

____

____

I Believe! I am Healed, Whole, and Worthy.

Symptom: Anxiety

At-Home Treatment: When panic and anxiety symptoms escalate into anxiety attacks and panic attacks, it may be an anxiety disorder. Anxiety disorders include generalized anxiety disorder, social anxiety, and panic disorder. Anxiety attacks and panic attack symptoms can be treated with medication and psychotherapy.

<u>Our Hope:</u> <u>Through It</u>

Scripture: *"When you pass through the waters, I will be with you; and through the rivers, they shall not overwhelm you; when you walk through fire you shall not be burned, and the flame shall not consume you."* Isaiah 43:2 NRSV

As you meditate on this verse from Isaiah 43, let it encourage you. The tide is about to change, what has been will no longer be, and you have made it through. Through the rivers, through the fire, but what you went through did not consume you. The Lord your God has walked with you as your protector, keeping your body, mind, and spirit intact. Your testimony is you do not look like what you've been through. Your mind has been stretched and stressed, but through it, you have learned to release those thoughts that would cause anxiety to build, to the Lord your God and even sought professional help, because Jesus and therapy work. Your body has felt everything you can name, and you've lost some weight unintentionally; but the aches, pains, nausea, the senses of taste and smell have begun to return. Your spirit has grown weary at times, it's been up and down, and through the downs, you have learned to call on the help of the Holy Spirit to lift you. You have put to practice the art of holding onto hope. The waters of the river did not overwhelm you, nor did the flame of the fire consume you. You have taken charge of this journey, speaking over yourself as confirmed in scripture, and that which you see in the spirit, and the Lord your God has kept the promise. You are not forsaken, but the Lord is with you every step of the way. You are healed, whole, and worthy.

Prayer:

Most gracious and eternal Lord, the Lord my God, thank you for covering and keeping me, through this trial, and its tests. Thank you for the power of the Holy Spirit, your healing touch, for walking with me and reminding me that I'm not alone, but you are with me. You are good and do good things. Let others see me and glorify you. In Jesus' name. Amen.

Honest Self-Assessment

Devotional Reflection:

____

____

____

____

____

____

____

How do you feel in body, mind, and spirit?

____

____

____

____

____

____

71

I Believe! I am Healed, Whole, and Worthy.

Symptom: Difficulty Breathing
At-Home Treatment: Seek Medical Help or Call 911

<u>Our Hope:</u> <u>Back and Better</u>

Scripture: *"For I will restore health to you,*
and your wounds I will heal, says the Lord..."
Jeremiah 30:17 NRSV

It is stated that the 30th chapter of Jeremiah is comprised of a collection of poetry and prose. Jeremiah was instructed to write concerning the new vision of both Israel and Judah. In the poetry God is the speaker, giving readers a new way of understanding life after trials.

When reading the 17th verse of this chapter, I became filled with joy, the excitement of knowing that God will restore. That God will bring you back to the places and spaces where you existed before; back into relationship with God, God's self, but also with those closest to you because you were an outcast. From the time you first began to feel symptoms, or when you were tested and received a positive result, you have been in isolation, cut off from the outside, confined to your personal space, with little to no visitors, and no interaction. By God's graceful hand on you, you have made it to the last day of the quarantine, and God is prepared to restore you. He's ready to bring you back, but this time, you're going to be better. While a man will look at the outward appearance God is looking at the internal things. This time has in no way been easy, and you have evolved. That is okay, in fact, it's great! Maybe before you didn't understand, but now it's beginning to make sense. Through your faithfulness, through your process, in devotion, meditation, and prayer, you have grown, matured in faith. You can identify where you are on your journey, accept it and do the work to want and experience better. Your spiritual voice has become more clear and sound, and you speak with the power you have been endowed with as a child, a daughter, a son of the Lord your God. Your outlook is optimistic and because of this, you are commanding the life you desire to the glory of God; your health restored and wounds healed. You are a healed, whole, and worthy; a living testimony.

72

Prayer:

To the God who restores my health, and heals my wounds, thank you. Thank you for touching my physical body, but also seeing past my exterior and searching my heart. For being with me those times I felt alone, sad, and struggled with my thoughts. Thank you that while I may have gone to places in my mind and felt things in my body, that I did not stay there long, but Lord, you brought me back. You are a restorer and as your child, I pray that my life exemplifies the grace that you've extended to me, as I extend grace to others, and myself. Thank you for the gift of life, the journey, my growth, and the good that shall come to me as a living witness, healed, whole, and worthy. It is in the great and mighty name of Jesus, I pray. Amen.

Honest Self-Assessment

Devotional Reflection:

____

____

____

____

____

____

____

How do you feel in body, mind, and spirit?

____

____

____

____

____

____

What are you speaking over yourself today?

I Believe! I am Healed, Whole, and Worthy.

And they overcame!

"And they overcame him, by the blood of the lamb and by the word of their testimony..." **Revelation 12:11 NKJV**

Our experience with COVID-19 was interesting. We noticed that our two-year-old daughter wasn't in her usual state of goofy and high energy. As a parent, we could see the sickness in her face and we tried to do everything we could to comfort her. Later that night she had an extremely high fever of 103. We took her to the ER and they diagnosed her with an ear infection and tested her for COVID. Our daughter getting tested is what prompted me to get tested. I knew in the back of my mind that if we're taking care of her and she has it then both my pregnant wife (at the time) and I both more than likely contracted it. My wife didn't bother getting tested. I ultimately don't know how we contracted it but when we found out we were positive, for a brief moment it was scary. It was scary because we would see on the news the rising death toll and how many others fought for their lives in ICU. By the grace of God, our symptoms were minor. Our two-year-old daughter bounced back a day after she received her results. My wife and I did lose our sense smell and taste and we were extremely fatigued for about a week. We were encouraged by our family, friends, and especially our church family. They prayed for us, dropped off groceries & care packages, called and checked on us, and assured us that we were not in this alone. That meant a lot! We believe we overcame it by the prayers of the people who prayed on our behalf and simply the Grace of God! We would say to someone experiencing, God is a healer! We are living witnesses! Keep the faith!

Troy Wilkins

My first symptom of Covid was a common cold for me, well at least I thought I was cold until I lost my appetite. The red flag for me was going to dialysis and by me losing my appetite I was losing weight and my dry weight was changing. On a normal day of dialysis, my dry weight is normally 121, it was dropping to 110. I was very fatigued, blood pressure dropped extremely low. I then realize maybe I should try to go to the ER. Went to the ER and the nurse was checking my vitals, she stated the symptoms sound like "Pneumonia "but we're going to give you a Covid test as well. 20 minutes went past and she came back with the results and said "I was tested positive for Covid". At that moment my emotions were everywhere, I was angry, sad, all the above. She said we're going to admit you and begin you on some antibiotics for the covid. I called my mother and told her the results of the test, she began to encourage me, I was so frustrated and defeated because I felt like God let me down. I then began I think about how did I get in contact with and induvial with Covid. I realized the weekend past I was at an event at a church, the individual was coughing and didn't have a mask. I immediately put it together that's was how I came in contact with the individual with Covid. I told a few of my family members and they all called me up and had a family prayer which encouraged me in so many ways. In my mind I was thinking having covid was a death sentence until I remember the God, I serve can overcome any sickness or pain. I can truly say how I got through this obstacle was God and my family!!! For anyone that may be going through covid right now. Don't allow that to be your death sentence, be encouraged and know that God can bring you out of anything.

Raina Corbin

My experience began after I let my guard down while helping a friend move furniture inside their home. Fortunately, my friend contacted me the next day to say that they had tested positive for COVID-19 that morning. My symptoms began two days after contact. Early symptoms were a headache and sore throat. I got tested, and confirmed positive, five days after contact. I did not feel as bad as I feared but the symptoms came and piled up. Felt like a new symptom each day. I experienced body aches, night sweats, headache, chest tightness, fatigue, eye pain, loss of taste, loss of smell, sinus pressure, nasal congestion, sneezing, coughing, and vertigo for roughly three weeks.

Initially, the thought of having COVID had me nervous. As I experienced it, I was fine "dealing" with all the symptoms as long as my lungs felt clear. Which, for the most part, they did. I developed bronchitis which was the cause of the chest tightness, but an x-ray found that there was no fluid/congestion. Knowing this gave me a sense of relief. My focus then shifted to staying positive to be mentally sharp and disciplined to do what I needed to get COVID behind me completely. Prayer, reading, stretching, and light exercise were part of my daily regimen. Even when I felt physically weak.

It's been months since I tested positive, and I am still feeling some effects from having COVID. Those issues include joint pain, occasional muscle ache, and fatigue. I learned that this is not that uncommon. Regardless of those lingering issues, I am faithful that my overall health will be restored. I would recommend that anyone who experiences COVID not panic but try to focus and lean into their faith as well as seek knowledge of how your body responds to diet, exercise, and supplements. Vitamins B12, C, D, E, Zinc, and ginger likely helped me a lot. Above all, God's will prevail. Trust that no matter what happens, He will guide you if you listen.

Vann Davis

I t could have been another way BUT God.

Where I was, is not where I should remain.

My declaration has NOT changed but I had to be reminded that what's coming is better than what has been. I BELIEVE IN GOD.

I AM HEALED, WHOLE and GOD has counted me WORTHY. While I may not be 100% yet, COMPLETE HEALING WILL BE MY PORTION.

"But He was wounded for our transgressions, He was bruised for our iniquities; The chastisement for our peace was upon Him, And by His stripes, we are healed." Isaiah 53:5 NKJV

and said, "If you diligently heed the voice of the Lord your God and do what is right in His sight, give ear to His commandments and keep all His statutes, I will put none of the diseases on you which I have brought on the Egyptians. For I am the Lord who heals you." Exodus 15:26 NKJV

I AM GRATEFUL AND BLESSED. God has been BETTER than GOOD to me.

"The blessing of the Lord makes one rich, And He adds no sorrow with it."

Proverbs 10:22 NKJV

"You have dealt well with Your servant, O Lord, according to Your word. Teach me good judgment and knowledge, For I believe Your commandments. Before I was afflicted, I went astray, but now I keep Your word. YOU ARE GOOD, AND DO GOOD; Teach me Your statutes." Psalm 119:65-68 NKJV

Cherish EVERY moment, Count EVERY blessing, and LIVE in the abundance of LIFE NOW. YOU DESERVE IT!

Rashad M. Roberts
Social Media Post December 7, 2020

As you Journey

Pray, Reflect, and Write

Today is______________(date)

Today I am grateful for:

____

____

____

____

____

____

____

Today I am working on:

____

____

____

____

____

____

____

Today I am affirming:

____

____

____

____

____

____

____

____

____

____

____

____

I Believe! I am Healed, Whole, and Worthy.

Today is________________(date)

Today I am grateful for:

____

____

____

____

____

____

Today I am working on:

____

____

____

____

____

Today I am affirming:

____

____

____

____

____

____

____

____

____

____

____

____

____

I Believe! I am Healed, Whole, and Worthy.

Today is_______________(date)

Today I am grateful for:

____

____

____

____

____

____

Today I am working on:

____

____

____

____

____

____

Today I am affirming:

I Believe! I am Healed, Whole, and Worthy.

Today is_______________(date)

Today I am grateful for:

____

____

____

____

____

____

____

Today I am working on:

____

____

____

____

____

____

Today I am affirming:

I Believe! I am Healed, Whole, and Worthy.

Today is_______________(date)

Today I am grateful for:

____

____

____

____

____

____

Today I am working on:

____

____

____

____

____

____

Today I am affirming:

I Believe! I am Healed, Whole, and Worthy.

Today is_______________(date)

Today I am grateful for:

____

____

____

____

____

____

____

Today I am working on:

____

____

____

____

____

____

Today I am affirming:

I Believe! I am Healed, Whole, and Worthy.

95

Today is________________(date)

Today I am grateful for:

____

____

____

____

____

____

____

Today I am working on:

____

____

____

____

____

____

Today I am affirming:

____

____

____

____

____

____

____

____

____

____

____

____

I Believe! I am Healed, Whole, and Worthy.

Today is_______________(date)

Today I am grateful for:

____

____

____

____

____

____

Today I am working on:

____

____

____

____

____

____

Today I am affirming:

I Believe! I am Healed, Whole, and Worthy.

Today is_______________(date)

Today I am grateful for:

____

____

____

____

____

____

____

Today I am working on:

____

____

____

____

____

____

____

Today I am affirming:

____

____

____

____

____

____

____

____

____

____

____

____

I Believe! I am Healed, Whole, and Worthy.

Today is______________(date)

Today I am grateful for:

____

____

____

____

____

____

____

Today I am working on:

____

____

____

____

____

____

Today I am affirming:

____

____

____

____

____

____

____

____

____

____

____

____

I Believe! I am Healed, Whole, and Worthy.

Today is_______________(date)

Today I am grateful for:

____

____

____

____

____

____

____

Today I am working on:

____

____

____

____

____

____

____

Today I am affirming:

____

____

____

____

____

____

____

____

____

____

____

____

I Believe! I am Healed, Whole, and Worthy.

Today is_______________(date)

Today I am grateful for:

____

____

____

____

____

____

Today I am working on:

____

____

____

____

____

____

Today I am affirming:

____

____

____

____

____

____

____

____

____

____

____

____

I Believe! I am Healed, Whole, and Worthy.

Today is_______________(date)

Today I am grateful for:

____

____

____

____

____

____

____

Today I am working on:

____

____

____

____

____

____

____

Today I am affirming:

____

____

____

____

____

____

____

____

____

____

____

____

I Believe! I am Healed, Whole, and Worthy.

Today is_______________(date)

Today I am grateful for:

____

____

____

____

____

____

____

Today I am working on:

____

____

____

____

____

____

____

Today I am affirming:

____

____

____

____

____

____

____

____

____

____

____

____

I Believe! I am Healed, Whole, and Worthy.

Today is_______________(date)

Today I am grateful for:

____

____

____

____

____

____

Today I am working on:

____

____

____

____

____

____

Today I am affirming:

____

____

____

____

____

____

____

____

____

____

____

____

I Believe! I am Healed, Whole, and Worthy.

Today is________________(date)

Today I am grateful for:

____

____

____

____

____

____

____

Today I am working on:

____

____

____

____

____

____

____

Today I am affirming:

____

____

____

____

____

____

____

____

____

____

____

____

I Believe! I am Healed, Whole, and Worthy.

Today is_______________(date)

Today I am grateful for:

____

____

____

____

____

____

Today I am working on:

____

____

____

____

____

____

Today I am affirming:

____

____

____

____

____

____

____

____

____

____

____

____

I Believe! I am Healed, Whole, and Worthy.

Today is_______________(date)

Today I am grateful for:

____

____

____

____

____

____

Today I am working on:

____

____

____

____

____

____

Today I am affirming:

I Believe! I am Healed, Whole, and Worthy.

Today is_______________(date)

Today I am grateful for:

____

____

____

____

____

____

____

Today I am working on:

____

____

____

____

____

____

____

Today I am affirming:

____

____

____

____

____

____

____

____

____

____

____

____

I Believe! I am Healed, Whole, and Worthy.

Today is______________(date)

Today I am grateful for:

____

____

____

____

____

____

Today I am working on:

____

____

____

____

____

____

Today I am affirming:

____

____

____

____

____

____

____

____

____

____

____

____

I Believe! I am Healed, Whole, and Worthy.

Today is_______________(date)

Today I am grateful for:

____

____

____

____

____

____

Today I am working on:

____

____

____

____

____

____

Today I am affirming:

____

____

____

____

____

____

____

____

____

____

____

____

I Believe! I am Healed, Whole, and Worthy.

Today is_______________(date)

Today I am grateful for:

____

____

____

____

____

____

____

Today I am working on:

____

____

____

____

____

____

Today I am affirming:

I Believe! I am Healed, Whole, and Worthy.

Today is_______________**(date)**

Today I am grateful for:

____

____

____

____

____

____

Today I am working on:

____

____

____

____

____

____

Today I am affirming:

I Believe! I am Healed, Whole, and Worthy.

129

Today is_______________(date)

Today I am grateful for:

____

____

____

____

____

____

____

Today I am working on:

____

____

____

____

____

____

Today I am affirming:

I Believe! I am Healed, Whole, and Worthy.

Today is_______________(date)

Today I am grateful for:

____

____

____

____

____

____

Today I am working on:

____

____

____

____

____

____

Today I am affirming:

____

____

____

____

____

____

____

____

____

____

____

____

I Believe! I am Healed, Whole, and Worthy.

Today is________________(date)

Today I am grateful for:

____

____

____

____

____

____

Today I am working on:

____

____

____

____

____

____

Today I am affirming:

I Believe! I am Healed, Whole, and Worthy.

Today is_______________(date)

Today I am grateful for:

____

____

____

____

____

____

Today I am working on:

____

____

____

____

____

____

Today I am affirming:

I Believe! I am Healed, Whole, and Worthy.

Today is_______________(date)

Today I am grateful for:

____

____

____

____

____

____

Today I am working on:

____

____

____

____

____

____

Today I am affirming:

____

____

____

____

____

____

____

____

____

____

____

I Believe! I am Healed, Whole, and Worthy.

Today is_______________(date)

Today I am grateful for:

____

____

____

____

____

____

Today I am working on:

____

____

____

____

____

____

Today I am affirming:

____

____

____

____

____

____

____

____

____

____

____

____

I Believe! I am Healed, Whole, and Worthy.

Today is_______________(date)

Today I am grateful for:

____

____

____

____

____

____

Today I am working on:

____

____

____

____

____

____

Today I am affirming:

____

____

____

____

____

____

____

____

____

____

____

____

I Believe! I am Healed, Whole, and Worthy.

I Believe! I am Healed, Whole, and Worthy.

I Believe! I am Healed, Whole, and Worthy.

I Believe! I am Healed, Whole, and Worthy.

I Believe! I am Healed, Whole, and Worthy.

149

I Believe! I am Healed, Whole, and Worthy.

I Believe! I am Healed, Whole, and Worthy.

I Believe! I am Healed, Whole, and Worthy.

I Believe! I am Healed, Whole, and Worthy.

I Believe! I am Healed, Whole, and Worthy.

I Believe! I am Healed, Whole, and Worthy.

I Believe! I am Healed, Whole, and Worthy.

I Believe! I am Healed, Whole, and Worthy.

I Believe! I am Healed, Whole, and Worthy.

I Believe! I am Healed, Whole, and Worthy.

I Believe! I am Healed, Whole, and Worthy.

I Believe! I am Healed, Whole, and Worthy.

I Believe! I am Healed, Whole, and Worthy.

I Believe! I am Healed, Whole, and Worthy.

I Believe! I am Healed, Whole, and Worthy.

I Believe! I am Healed, Whole, and Worthy.

I Believe! I am Healed, Whole, and Worthy.

I Believe! I am Healed, Whole, and Worthy.

I Believe! I am Healed, Whole, and Worthy.

I Believe! I am Healed, Whole, and Worthy.

I Believe! I am Healed, Whole, and Worthy.

THANK YOU

Thank you to my family, church family, and friends for your prayers, and presence through my time with covid. Love you all.

A special thank you, to the staff of both INOVA Hospital and INOVA Transitional Services of Alexandria, Virginia. From intake to discharge, and even my continued care, your professionalism, expertise, and encouragement are greatly appreciated.

This work is dedicated to every individual that has contracted covid-19 over the last two years and survived, as well as the countless lives of more than 6 million worldwide, and 957K in the United States that have passed, including family and friends. May God grant you and your loved one's comfort, peace, and strength to journey on. In addition, this work is dedicated to those who may contract covid in the future and because of faith and science have a greater chance of survival.